HOW TO IMPROVE YOUR THOUGHTS

Practical tips to improve your thoughts and to achieve a better life

Dr April H. Bejarano

Table of contents

Chapter 1

How to know yourself well

You are stardust that in some way woke up, and how and why that happened is a secret. So the inquiry is, Where did that stardust come from and how could it become alive?
The universe was made 13.7 quite a while back in a moment called the Big Bang.*** No one knows how or why the Big Bang occurred, or how or why life came to exist on Earth. Notwithstanding, science keeps on bettering comprehend the circumstances that were available at those times. From the start, the universe was more modest than a molecule, was unimaginably hot, and contained everything in the present universe. The universe then extended at unimaginable

speed and inside the primary second energy broke into the powers of electromagnetism and gravity. Then, at that point, cncrgy solidified to frame matter. 380,000 years after the Big Bang the main particles showed up as enormous billows of hydrogen and helium. Those mists had a temperature distinction of only 1/1,000 of a degree, which was barely enough for gravity to begin compacting those mists.

As those mists compacted their thickness expanded, which made gravity become all the more impressive; and as gravity turned out to be all the more remarkable the temperatures in the mists rose. At the point when temperatures at last rose to 10 million degrees, protons began to intertwine, which delivered a gigantic measure of energy that made billions of stars structure all through the universe.

In any case, those new stars at last kicked the bucket, and as they were biting the dust their temperatures climbed so high that the protons in them melded into particles of different components like carbon, oxygen, nitrogen, sodium, gold, and so forth. Also, when those stars at long last passed on they detonated, which dispersed the residue of those components across the universe. Simultaneously as those old stars were kicking the bucket and detonating new, youthful stars were shaping and the residue from the dead, detonated stars began whirling around the new stars. That twirling dust then, at that point, consolidated to shape minute particles and little pieces of rock that ultimately joined to frame space rocks, planets, and moons as displayed in the above photograph of universe M106 by the Hubble Space Telescope.

That is the manner by which our Earth and nearby planet group were shaped 4.5 quite a while back. Dust that had been dissipated across the universe by detonating, dead stars began whirling around another star, our Sun. That dust then, at that point, joined into increasingly large pieces, which then, at that point, consolidated to frame Earth and different planets and different moons and space rocks around us. Furthermore, as it turned out Earth had the perfect blend of energy, compound components, and water for life to shape. Today your body is comprised of the residue of that equivalent carbon, oxygen, nitrogen, sodium, gold, and so forth that was dispersed across the universe by detonating stars billions of years prior.

Stardust Comes Alive: Life needs energy, yet not an excessive amount of energy or excessively little. In the focal point of a star, there is such a lot of energy (heat) that any particles that really do consolidate promptly get busted separated by the intensity. In intergalactic space, there is so little energy (cold) that particles can't join since it is excessively cold. What is required for life is a perfectly measured proportion of energy, and Earth has a perfectly measured proportion of energy since we are close, yet not excessively close, to the Sun.

Life additionally needs numerous synthetic components and it needs a fluid like water. Why a fluid? Since iotas in gasses move past one another so quick that they can't consolidate. What's more, in solids, particles are stuck so firmly together that they can't move around and join. In fluids, particles are allowed to move around and connect up to frame the atoms that are fundamental forever.

The Earth shaped 4.5 quite a while back and it had practically ideal circumstances for life to frame. It was the perfect separation from our star the Sun to contain immense expanses of untamed water. Furthermore, far below those seas at breaks in the Earth's hull, there was both intensity leaking up from inside the Earth and an extraordinary variety of components. So at those hot breaks somewhere down in the seas phenomenal science started to occur, which empowered iotas to join into a wide range of extraordinary mixes. Life is something other than colorful science, notwithstanding. For life to exist expected that the immense particles that were shaping somewhere down in the sea become steady and duplicate. Some way or another 3.8 quite a while back those enormous particles became steady and they began to repeat, yet nobody knows how or why that occurred. Nobody knows how or why life on Earth came to exist. What we can be sure of is that while the energy in our universe pushes toward entropy (scatters) as per the second law of thermodynamics, our universe is likewise ready to change itself toward a path that is positive, moderate, and perpetually complicated.

We don't have any idea why the universe is constantly changing in this certain, moderate, always complex heading, yet obviously, this change keeps on happening directly before us consistently.

Life Learned How To Learn: Again, for life to exist required the colossal atoms shaping somewhere down in the sea to become steady and imitate. Those steady particles of life that framed somewhere down in the sea and figured out how to duplicate themselves 3.8 quite a while back are called DNA. A DNA particle is comprised of a twofold helix associated by rungs, and it contains all the data important to replicate itself. At the point when you cut yourself and afterward it mends, that happens on the grounds that your dna has recreated itself consequently without you doing anything. Who Am I DNA Molecule: The DNA of people (additionally called our genome) contains 6 billion pieces of data. 99.9% of that data is a similar in each individual. As it were .1% of that data changes, which is the reason we are marginally not quite the same as each other. DNA doesn't necessarily in every case replicate itself and its data precisely, be that as it may - it has defects. As DNA duplicates itself, once in each billion replications there will in general be a mistake. A portion of that DNA with blunders wind up working and consequently become new sorts of the living organic entity. Also, those new kinds of living creatures with blunders then, at that point, begin rivaling their unique parent DNA for assets, and whichever variant wins those assets is the one in particular that gets by. Through such interior blunders of replicating itself DNA aggregates new data about what works best in its conditions, and in this manner it figures out how to more readily adjust to the conditions wherein it tracks down itself.

The primary types of life that showed up on Earth 3.8 a long time back were basic, single cells like these:

Stromatolites Version 2: These are your most established living distant grandparents. They are lichen called cyanobacteria developing here on dead clusters of themselves called Stromatolites. Cyanobacteria originally appeared around 3.5 quite a while back and they are the second most established daily routine structure to have at any point experienced on Earth. Botches made as the DNA of cyanobacteria duplicated itself delivered the vast majority of life on Earth today. As the DNA in those single cells reproduced itself, those cells learned through such DNA replication blunders how to all the more likely adjust to their conditions, and through that cycle, the cells turned out to be more different and complex. Then beginning around 600 to quite a while back this experimentation cycle of DNA learning came about in multi-celled creatures like growths, fish, plants, amphibia, reptiles, and dinosaurs.

During that time DNA was likewise having blunders that brought about quicker approaches to learning, and that cycle ultimately brought about living beings with minds that learned continuously. Anyway when those creatures with minds kicked the bucket the data that gathered in their cerebrum passed on with them.

Then, at that point, quite a while back a space rock struck Earth close to the Yucatan Peninsula making conditions comparable to those of an atomic conflict, which cleared out the dinosaurs. The shortfall of dinosaurs left specialties on Earth in which the precursors of people could prosper thus DNA then figured out how to change itself into people.

As yet unchanged Old Mystery The above segments depict how science sees the circumstances that were available when and since stardust and life appeared. You should see anyway that neither researchers nor any other person know HOW and WHY stardust and life appeared. How and why stardust and life appeared stays a secret.

However you are right here - stardust that in some way woke up - perusing these words while drifting through perpetual space on a bit of soil and water encompassed by an extremely, meager layer of air. The possibilities of that steadily happening were way, way, far past tiny.

Many individuals today guarantee that this secret is presently not a secret but instead that this secret is effectively settled just by taking on their convictions, which they guarantee are valid. However such obvious convictions about this secret have quite often caused divisions in the public arena and separateness in people. Humanity has consistently held this secret to be what is generally sacrosanct and blessed to us. Further, for the vast majority, this secret rouses wonder, stunningness, respect, and appreciation, and for some a need to communicate those sentiments. You can communicate your sentiments about this secret and completely celebrate existence without looking unendingly for genuine convictions, which you won't ever find. All things being equal, you can basically acknowledge that this secret is a secret to you, which then, at that point, permits you to unwind, be content and continue ahead with life.

Chapter 2

Get rid of negative thoughts in life

Quite possibly of the greatest test individuals face today is remaining hopeful.

We are living in the midst of large changes and are besieged day to day with awful news; stories that influence us and effect our desire for the decency of humanity. We can become involved with the rush of antagonism the media grandstands. It presents to us an oblivious sensation of solace when we think, "Essentially that didn't occur to me, right?"

This is certainly not a positive outlook for mentors. As mentors, we are adequately fortunate to have the right stuff accessible to improve others' lives. We have the ability to change pessimism to energy, each client in turn. Mentors should go forward into the future to make our reality a spot where uplifting news, not terrible, is the norm. To accomplish this, we should be hopeful about our opportunities for progress. Without positive thinking, we can't push ahead.

Step by step instructions to prepare yourself to have a hopeful attitude

The psyche capabilities as a repository, and we should figure out how to supply this supply. Good faith is an attributive style; basically, a way we trait significance to everyday occasions.

While assessing an unavoidable truth, skeptical people and hopeful people will have inverse viewpoints of one another.

For a Positive Fact: "I received a pay increase!"

Hopeful Profile: Everything generally turns out for me. Worrier Profile: My expenses will be significantly higher at this point. For a negative truth: "I lost my home keys." Optimistic Profile: Dilemma nothing, somebody presumably got them for me. Worrier Profile: I generally fail to remember everything; I am so diverted! In the event that you end up relating to the worry wart profile, be encouraged. With mental strength and day to day preparing, you will actually want to cause great in any circumstance.

Beginning with your discourse, dispose of negative expressions, for example, "I can't", "I generally surrender", or "I'm *insert negative descriptive word For instance, you might have wound up saying, "I'm languid." A superior method for outlining this to you is "Today I didn't achieve however much I needed to. I will make a rundown for later so I can finish my errands as a whole!" Additionally, attempt to abstain from griping no matter what. In the event that you are working with an especially troublesome client, attempt to see the experience as a positive test as opposed to a negative circumstance. This will permit you to stay feeling great and help the client in the most potential useful manner.

One more method for preparing your mind to be more hopeful is by keep positive occasions in your day, regardless of how littlc. Assuming you brought down the anxiety of a philanthropic director, record that in your diary. In the event that you pass an especially gorgeous nursery, snap a photo or make a note. On the off chance that you have a useful discussion with your group, track the features. By doing this, you will prepare yourself to zero in on the up-sides around you. Furthermore, consistently, ensure you keep an open attitude to finding out about and rehearsing good faith. It is difficult, however with difficult work and constancy, you will actually want to stay hopeful despite cynicism.

Instructing for social advancement requests that we accomplish the difficult work to have an effect. We are working with clients who could acquire significant advantages from our administrations, however who might have never even known about instructing. We are working with philanthropies that are handling the absolute hardest and most significant issues of today. With confidence in our souls and brains, we can stroll into the war zone of life consistently prepared to make positive change.

Additionally, Negative reasoning seems, by all accounts, to be more common than positive reasoning. It appears to be that with the vast majority, positive reasoning requires some work, while, negative reasoning comes effectively, and is frequently excluded. This has a lot of to do with training and the climate one has been living in. Assuming that you have been raised in a cheerful and positive climate, there is greater likelihood that it will be simpler for you to decidedly think. Nonetheless, If you have been raised in poor or tough spots, you will all the more most likely be leaned to negative reasoning.

We view the world through our transcendent mental disposition. Assuming our considerations are positive, that is finc, however in the event that they are negative, our life and conditions would presumably reflect these negative contemplations. Assuming you accept that you will fall flat, you could unwittingly attack each an amazing open door to succeed. Assuming you are excessively short of meeting new individuals, or abstain from having cozy connections, you will do all that to keep away from individuals and connections, and afterward grumble that you are desolate and no one loves you. Rather than turning out to be more certain and defeating your feelings of dread, you ponder that it is so hard to succeed or to interface with individuals, and you hope to desolate be a disappointment or remain.

The Power of Negative Thinking In Action Do you frequently ponder hardships, disappointment, and fiascos?

Do you continue to ponder the negative news you see and hear on TV or read about in the papers? Do you see yourself adhered and incapable to work on your life or your wellbeing? Do you regularly feel that you don't merit satisfaction or cash, or that getting them is excessively troublesome? On the off chance that you do, you will close your brain, see no open doors, and act and respond in such ways, as to repulse individuals and open doors. Frequently, the psyche doesn't pass judgment or look at contemplations and sentiments prior to tolerating them. In the event that what it hears, sees, and peruses is consistently regrettable, it acknowledges cynicism as the standard attitude. Positive Thinking pin: Discover How to Create a Positive Mindset

The media continually barrages the brain with a ton of data about fiascos, disasters, wars, and other troubled occasions. This data sinks into your psyche brain, and afterward, appears as your ongoing way of reasoning. It is alright to watch and hear the news since you want to realize what's going on the planet. In any case, be mindful so as not to exaggerate that. Bc mindful so as not to let what you hear and see on the news influence you to an extreme.

Assuming you consume the brain with discouraging and critical contemplations you transmit negative energy into the encompassing scene, and thusly, make and reproduce greater cynicism, disappointment, and calamities. The psyche is impartial energy. The manner in which you think decides if the outcomes are positive and helpful, or unsafe. It is a similar energy acting in various ways. Fortunately persevering inward work can address propensities for thinking. You should invest effort and time to seek after sure reasoning, to change your psychological disposition. The force of negative reasoning is areas of strength for very, with some work on your part, you can conquer it.

Basic Tips to Overcome Negative Thinking: Here are a couple of tips to assist you with staying away from negative reasoning: Every time you find yourself thinking a negative idea, supplant it with a positive one. Assuming you find yourself envisioning disappointment, quickly imagine accomplishment all things being equal.

Assuming that you hear yourself involving negative words in your discussion, change to positive words. Rather than saying, "I can't", say, "I can". More often than not you can, yet decide to say "can't", because of dread, sluggishness, or absence of confidence. Do you rehash negative words and expressions to you? Transform them to positive ones. Indeed, this expects you to be more ready and to invest some energy. You need to change negative reasoning into positive reasoning, isn't that right? Permit more uplifting perspective into your life. Have more confidence in yourself and anticipate positive outcomes. Confirmations and perception can steer you quite far toward this path. Conclude that from today, from this exact second, you are abandoning negative reasoning you, and beginning the way toward positive reasoning and conduct.

Negative reasoning incredibly affects everybody's life. It prompts disappointment, despondency, and absence of fulfillment, to stresses, and fears. In any case, there is not a great explanation to allow it to influence your life. You can liberate yourself from it by following the tips proposed here. The force of negative reasoning is a strong power that influences everybody. You should know about it and stop it at whatever point you wind up letting it penetrates into your brain and your contemplations. It is a propensity for the psyche, and frequently it is areas of strength for a. In any case, you can dispose of it, through sure reasoning and making a positive move.

Chapter 3

Increasing positive thinking

It is a decision to Have an inspirational perspective. You can decide to think considerations that raise your state of mind, toss an additional useful light on tough spots, and for the most part variety your day with more brilliant, more confident ways to deal with the things you do. By deciding to take an inspirational perspective on life, you can start to move out of a negative mood and see life as loaded up with potential outcomes and arrangements rather than stresses and impediments. If you have any desire to know how to think all the more decidedly, simply follow these tips. Evaluating Your Thinking: Take liability regarding your mentality. You are exclusively liable for your viewpoints, and your point of view is a choice.[1] If you will generally think adversely, you are deciding to maintain that viewpoint.

With training, you can decide to have a more sure outlook.[2] Comprehend the advantages of being a positive scholar. Deciding to think all the more emphatically won't just assist you with assuming command over your life and make your regular encounters more lovely, yet it can likewise help your psychological and actual wellbeing as well as your capacity to manage change. Monitoring these advantages can assist you with being much more inspired to think emphatically regularly.[3]Here are a few advantages of positive reasoning: An expanded life expectancy Lower paces of sadness and pain

More noteworthy protection from the normal virus Better mental and actual prosperity

Better adapting abilities during seasons of pressure A more inherent capacity to shape connections and concrete bonds Keep a journal to mirror your contemplations. Recording your contemplations can empower you to step back and assess designs in your reasoning. Record your contemplations and sentiments and attempt to recognize any triggers that lead to one or the other positive or negative considerations. Requiring only twenty minutes to understand your thought process toward the finish of each and every day can be an important method for recognizing your negative contemplations and make an arrangement to transform them to positive considerations.

Your diary can take on any structure that you like. On the off chance that you don't want to compose verbose intelligent passages, you can simply make a rundown of the five most common negative contemplations and positive considerations you had that day. Make certain to offer yourself the time and chance to assess and consider the data in the diary. Assuming that you compose consistently, you might need to reflect toward the finish of each and every week. Battling Negative Thoughts:

Identify your programmed negative contemplations. To move away from the negative reasoning that is keeping you away from having an uplifting perspective, you'll have to turn out to be more mindful of your "programmed negative considerations". At the point when you remember them, you're in a situation to challenge them and provide them their walking requests to move right out of your head.[4] An illustration of a programmed negative idea is, after hearing that you have a forthcoming test, you think, "I'll most likely bomb it." The idea is programmed in light of the fact that it's your underlying response to catching wind of the test. Challenge your negative considerations. Regardless of whether you have gone through the majority of your time on earth thinking adversely, you don't need to keep being negative. Whenever you have a negative thought, especially a programmed negative idea, pause and assess whether the idea is valid or accurate.[5]

One method for testing negative contemplations is to be evenhanded. Record the negative idea and contemplate how you would answer if another person said the idea to you. You could almost certainly offer an objective reply to another person's pessimism, regardless of whether you track down it hard to accomplish for yourself.[6] For instance, you might have the pessimistic thought, "I generally bomb tests." It is far-fetched that you would in any case be in school assuming you generally bomb tests. Revisit your records or grades and find tests that you got a passing grade on; these test the negative idea. You might try and find that you have tests that you passed with As and Bs, which would additionally affirm that your cynicism is misrepresented. Supplant the negative contemplations with positive considerations. When you're feeling sure that you can recognize and challenge pessimistic contemplations, you're prepared to settle on dynamic decisions about supplanting pessimistic considerations with good ones. This doesn't imply that all that in your life will constantly be positive; having different emotions is typical. Notwithstanding, you can attempt to supplant the everyday pointless reasoning examples with considerations that assist you with prospering. For instance, assuming that you have the thought, "I will most likely bomb the test," stop yourself. You've proactively distinguished the idea as negative and assessed its exactness. Presently take a stab at supplanting it with a positive idea. A positive idea doesn't need to be indiscriminately hopeful, for example, "I will get a 100 on the test, regardless of whether I review." It can be something as straightforward as, "I will set aside some margin to review and get ready so I excel on the test as I can."

Utilize the force of inquiries. At the point when you pose your cerebrum an inquiry, it will in general track down the response for you. In the event that you ask yourself, "For what reason is life so horrendous?" your cerebrum will attempt to address your inquiry. The equivalent is valid assuming that you ask yourself, "How could I become so fortunate?". Ask yourself inquiries that draw your concentration onto positive contemplations. Limit outside impacts that animate your pessimism. You might find that particular sorts of music or savage computer games or motion pictures impact your in general attitude.[7] Try limiting your openness to unpleasant or rough upgrades and invest more energy paying attention to quieting music or perusing. Music helps your psyche well and books on sure reasoning can give great tips to being a more joyful individual.

Stay away from "highly contrasting reasoning." In this sort of reasoning, otherwise called "polarizing," all that you experience either is or alternately isn't; there are no shades of dim. This can lead individuals to feel like they need to accomplish something impeccably or not at all.[8]

To stay away from this sort of reasoning, embrace the shades of dim throughout everyday life. Rather than thinking with regards to two results (one sure and one negative), make a rundown of every one of the in the middle between to see that things aren't quite as desperate as they appear. For instance, on the off chance that you have a test coming up and feel really awkward with the topic, you might be enticed to not step through the exam or to not read up for it by any stretch of the imagination, so on the off chance that you fizzle, this is on the grounds that you didn't actually attempt. Notwithstanding, this is overlooking the way that you're probably going to improve assuming you invest more energy getting ready for the test.

You ought to likewise try not to believe that the main results of your test-taking are An or a F. There is a great deal of "hazy situation" between the An and the F. Stay away from "customizing". Customizing is expccting that you are actually to fault for whatever turns out badly. Assuming you take this kind of reasoning excessively far, you can get suspicious and imagine that nobody likes you or needs to spend time with you and that every last move you make will dishearten someone.[9] Somebody who is customizing may think, "Betty didn't grin at me toward the beginning of today. I probably effectively resentful her." However, all things considered, Betty was simply having a terrible day, and her mind-set didn't have anything to do with you. Keep away from "channel thinking." This is the point at which you decide to hear the negative side of a circumstance as it were. Most circumstances have components that are both great and awful, and it assists with perceiving both. On the off chance that you hold this view, you won't ever see the positive in any situation.[10] For instance, you might step through an exam and get a C, alongside input from your educator saying that your presentation improved enormously from the last test. Sifting can make you just ponder the C and disregard the way that you have shown improvement and development.

Keep away from "catastrophizing." This is the point at which you expect that the absolute worst result is going to happen.[11] Catastrophizing is typically connected with nervousness about performing ineffectively. You can battle catastrophizing by being sensible about the potential results of a circumstance. For instance, you could feel that you will bomb a test you've been reading up for. A catastrophizer will then, at that point, stretch out that frailty to expect that you'll then, at that point, bomb the class and need to exit school, then end up jobless and on government assistance. Assuming you're reasonable about adverse results, you'll understand that regardless of whether you were to bomb a test, it's far-fetched that you would fundamentally bomb the course, and you wouldn't need to exit school.

Keep away from individuals who sap your energy and inspiration. In the event that you can't stay away from them or don't have any desire to, figure out how not to allow them to get you down and keep your association with them brief.

Try not to date anybody with a negative standpoint. In the event that you're as of now inclined to negative reasoning, you'll be falling into a snare. On the off chance that you truly do end up involved with somebody who battles to think emphatically, however, looking for advising together may be your most ideal choice.

Chapter 4

How to Stop worrying yourself

Is it safe to say that you are tormented by steady concerns and feelings of apprehension? These tips can assist with quieting your stressed brain and straightforwardness tension. How much stressing is excessively?

Stresses, questions, and tensions are a typical piece of life. It's normal to stress over a neglected bill, an impending prospective employee meeting, or a first date. Be that as it may, "typical" stress becomes unreasonable when it's industrious and wild. You stress consistently over "what uncertainties" and most pessimistic scenario situations, you can't get feelings of apprehension somewhere far away from me, and it slows down your regular routine.

Consistent stressing, pessimistic reasoning, and continuously expecting the most exceedingly terrible can negatively affect your profound and actual wellbeing. It can drain your profound strength, leave you feeling fretful and unsteady, cause sleep deprivation, migraines, stomach issues, and muscle pressure, and make it challenging to amass at work or school. You might take your gloomy sentiments out on individuals nearest to you, self-cure with liquor or medications, or attempt to occupy yourself by daydreaming before screens. Constant stressing can likewise be a significant side effect of Generalized Anxiety Disorder (GAD), a typical uneasiness problem that includes pressure, anxiety, and a general sensation of disquiet that colors for what seems like forever. On the off chance that you're tormented by misrepresented stress and pressure, there are steps you can take to switch off fears. Constant stressing is a psychological propensity that can be broken. You can prepare your cerebrum

to keep even-tempered and check out at life from a more adjusted, less unfortunate viewpoint.
For what reason is it so difficult to quit stressing? Steady stressing can incur significant damage. It can keep you up around evening time and make you tense and restless during the day. Furthermore, despite the fact that you disdain feeling like a worry wort, it can in any case be so hard to stop. For most persistent worriers, the fears are filled by the convictions — both negative and positive — that you hold about stressing:
Negative convictions about stress. You might accept that your steady stressing is destructive, that making you insane or influence your actual health is going. Or on the other hand you might stress that you will lose all command over your stressing — that it won't dominate and ever stop. While negative convictions, or agonizing over stressing, adds to your uneasiness and keep stressed going, positive convictions about stressing can

similarly as harm. Positive convictions about stress. You might accept that your stressing assists you with keeping away from terrible things, forestalls issues, sets you up for the most awful, or prompts arrangements. Perhaps you let yourself that know if you continue to stress over an issue sufficiently long, you'll ultimately have the option to sort it out. Or on the other hand maybe you're persuaded that stressing is something mindful to do or the best way to guarantee you don't ignore something? It's difficult to get out from under the concern propensity assuming that you trust that your stressing fills a positive need. When you understand that stressing is the issue, not the arrangement, you can recapture control of your stressed psyche. The most effective method to quit stressing tip 1: Create a day to day "stress" period It's difficult to be useful in your everyday exercises when nervousness and stress are overwhelming your contemplations and diverting you from work, school, or your home life. This is where the technique of delaying stressing can help. Instead of attempting to stop or dispose of a fear, license yourself to have it, however put off harping on it until some other time. Make a "stress period." Choose a set setting for stressing. It ought to be a similar consistently (for example in the family room from 5:00 to 5:20 p.m.) and early enough that it won't make you restless just before sleep time. During your concern period, you're permitted to stress over anything that's at the forefront of your thoughts. The remainder of the day, notwithstanding, is a straightforward zone.

Record your concerns. In the event that a fear or stress comes into your head during the day, make a concise note of it and afterward go on about your day. Advise yourself that have opportunity and willpower to consider it later, so there's compelling reason need to stress over it at the present time. Likewise, recording your contemplations — on a cushion or your telephone or PC — is a lot harder work than essentially suspecting them, so your concerns are bound to lose their power. Go over your "stress list" during the concern time frame. Assuming the considerations you recorded are as yet irritating you, permit yourself to stress over them, however just for how much time you've determined for your concern period. As you look at your concerns along these lines, you'll frequently find it simpler to foster a more adjusted viewpoint. What's more, on the off chance that your concerns don't appear to be significant any longer, essentially cut your concern period off and partake in the remainder of your day.

Tip 2: Challenge genuine fears: If you experience the ill effects of ongoing tension and stress, odds are you take a gander at the world in manners that cause it to appear to be more compromising than it is. For instance, you might misjudge the likelihood that things will turn out severely, hop promptly to most pessimistic scenario situations, or treat each genuine fear as though it were reality. You may likewise ruin your capacity to deal with life's concerns, accepting you'll self-destruct at the earliest difficult situation. These kinds of considerations, known as mental twists, include: All-or-nothing thinking, seeing things in dark or-white classes, with no center ground. "In the event that everything is more than a little flawed, I'm an all out disappointment. Overgeneralization from a solitary negative encounter, anticipating that it should hold for eternity. "I didn't land employed for the position. I won't ever land any position. Zeroing in on the negatives while sifting through the up-sides. Seeing the one thing that turned out badly, instead of the relative multitude of things that went right. "I triumphed ultimately the keep going inquiry on the test wrong.

I'm a blockhead. Concocting justifications for why positive occasions don't count. "I excelled on the show, yet that was simply blind chance. Making negative understandings without genuine proof. You carry on like telepathic: "I can see she subtly despises me." Or a spiritualist: "I simply know something horrible will occur. Anticipate that the worst situation imaginable should occur. "The pilot expressed we're in for some disturbance. The plane will crash Believing that the manner in which you feel reflects reality. "I feel like such a nitwit. Everybody should be snickering at me. Holding yourself to a severe rundown of what you ought to and shouldn't do and whipping yourself in the event that you disrupt any of the norms. "I ought to never have taken a stab at beginning a discussion with her. I'm such a bonehead. Naming yourself in light of errors and seen weaknesses. "I'm a disappointment; I'm exhausting; I should be distant from everyone else. Taking care of things that are unchangeable as far as you might be concerned. "It's my issue my child got in a mishap. I ought to have cautioned him to drive cautiously in the downpour. The fact that the idea is valid makes how to challenge these contemplations During your concern period, challenge your negative considerations by asking yourself: What the proof? That it's false? Is there a more sure, reasonable perspective on circumstance? What's the likelihood that what I'm frightened of will occur? Assuming the likelihood is low, what are a few additional logical results? Is the idea supportive? How might agonizing over it assist me and how with willing it hurt me?

What might I share with a this companion stress?

Tip 3: Distinguish among feasible and unsolvable concerns Research shows that while you're stressing, you briefly feel less restless. Running over the issue in your mind diverts you from your feelings and causes you to feel like you're getting something achieved. In any case, stressing and critical thinking are two totally different things. Critical thinking includes assessing what is happening, concocting substantial strides for managing it, and afterward setting the strategy in motion. Stressing, then again, seldom prompts arrangements. Regardless of how long you activity. Stressing, then again, seldom prompts arrangements. Regardless of how long you spend harping on most pessimistic scenario situations, you're not any more ready to manage them would it be advisable for them they occur. Is your concern feasible? Useful, feasible concerns are those you can make a move on immediately. For instance, assuming you're stressed over your bills, you could call your leasers to see about adaptable installment choices. Useless, unsolvable concerns are those for which there is no relating activity. "Consider the possibility that I get malignant growth sometime in the future?" or "Imagine a scenario in which my child gets into a mishap?" If the concern is reasonable, begin conceptualizing. Create a rundown of the relative multitude of potential arrangements you can imagine. Do whatever it takes not to get too hung up on tracking down the ideal arrangement. Center around the things you have the ability to change, as opposed to the conditions or real factors outside of your reach. After you've assessed your choices, make an arrangement of activity. When you have an arrangement and begin taking care of the issue, you'll feel considerably less restless. In the event that the concern isn't reasonable, acknowledge the vulnerability. In the event that you're a persistent worrier, by far most of your genuine fears presumably fall in this camp. Stressing is in many cases a way we attempt to foresee what's to come has in the store-a method for forestalling disagreeable shocks and control the result. The issue is, it doesn't work. Contemplating everything that could turn out badly doesn't make life any more unsurprising. Zeroing in on most pessimistic scenario situations will just hold you back from partaking in the beneficial things you have in the present.

To quit stressing, tackle your requirement for conviction and prompt responses. Do you will quite often foresee awful things will happen on the grounds that they are dubious? What is the probability they will? Given the probability is exceptionally low, is it conceivable to live with the little opportunity that something negative might occur? Ask your loved ones how they adapt to vulnerability in unambiguous circumstances. Might you at any point do likewise? Tune into your feelings. Stressing over vulnerability is in many cases a method for staying away from undesirable feelings. However, by tuning into your feelings you can begin to acknowledge your sentiments, even those that are awkward or don't appear to be legit.

Tip 4: Interrupt the concern cycle: If you stress unnecessarily, it can seem like negative contemplations are going through your mind on perpetual rehash. You might feel like you're spiraling wild, going off the deep end, or going to wear out under the heaviness of this tension. Yet, there are steps you can take right now to intrude on that large number of genuine concerns and give yourself a break from tireless stressing. Get up and get going. Practice is a characteristic and compelling enemy of nervousness treatment since it discharges endorphins which ease strain and stress, support energy, and upgrade your feeling of prosperity. Significantly more critically, by truly zeroing in on how your body feels as you move, you can interfere with the consistent progression of stresses going through your mind. Focus on the impression of your feet raising a ruckus around town as you walk, run, or dance, for instance, the cadence of your breathing, or the sensation of the sun or wind on your skin. Take a yoga or judo class. By zeroing in your brain on your developments and breathing, rehearsing yoga or judo keeps your consideration on the present, assisting with clearing your psyche and lead to a casual state. Ponder. Contemplation works by changing your concentration from stressing over the future or choosing not to move on to what's going on the present moment. By being completely taken part in the current second, you can intrude on the unending circle of negative considerations and stresses. What's more, you don't have to sit leg over leg, light candles or incense, or serenade. Essentially track down a calm, agreeable spot and pick one of the many free or modest cell phone applications that can direct you through the reflection cycle. Practice moderate muscle unwinding. This can assist you with breaking the perpetual circle of stressing by zeroing in your brain on your body rather than your viewpoints. By on the other hand straining and afterward delivering different muscle bunches in your body, you discharge muscle pressure in your body. Furthermore, as your body unwinds, your psyche will follow.

Attempt profound relaxing. At the point when you stress, you become restless and inhale quicker, frequently prompting further tension. Be that as it may, by rehearsing profound breathing activities, you can quiet your psyche and calm negative contemplations. Unwinding procedures can change the mind

While the above unwinding strategies can give some quick relief from stress and nervousness, rehearsing them consistently can likewise change your cerebrum. Research has shown that ordinary contemplation, for instance, can support movement on the left half of the prefrontal cortex, the region of the cerebrum answerable for sensations of quietness and bliss. The more you practice, the more prominent the nervousness help you'll insight and the more control you'll begin to feel over your anxieties and stresses.

Tip 5: Talk about your concerns It might appear to be an oversimplified arrangement, yet talking up close and personal with a confided in companion or relative — somebody who will pay attention to you without judging, censuring, or consistently being diverted — is one of the best ways of quieting your sensory system and diffuse uneasiness. At the point when your concerns begin spiraling, talking them over can cause them to appear to be undeniably less compromising. Hushing up about stresses just objective them to develop until they appear to be overpowering. Yet, expressing them without holding back can frequently assist you with getting a handle on the thing you're feeling and put things in context. Assuming that your apprehensions are ridiculous, expressing them can uncover them for what they are — unnecessary concerns. What's more, assuming your feelings of trepidation are legitimate, imparting them to another person can create arrangements that you might not have considered alone. Construct major areas of strength for a framework. People are social animals. We're not intended to live in disengagement. Be that as it may, serious areas of strength for a framework doesn't be guaranteed to mean a huge organization of companions. Try not to misjudge the advantage of a couple of individuals you can trust and rely on to show up for you. Furthermore, in the event that you don't feel that you have anybody to trust in, building new friendships is rarely past the point of no return. Know who to keep away from while you're feeling restless. Your restless interpretation of life might be something you realized when you were growing up. In the event that your mom is a persistent worrier, she isn't the most ideal individual to call while you're feeling restless — regardless of how close you are. While thinking about who to go to, find out if you will more often than not feel significantly improved or more awful in the wake of conversing with that individual about an issue.

Tip 6: Practice care: Worrying is generally centered around the future — on what could occur and what you'll do about it — or on the past, reiterating the things you've said or done. The exceptionally old act of care can assist you with breaking liberated from your concerns by taking your consideration back to the present. This methodology depends on noticing your concerns and afterward letting them go, assisting you with recognizing where your reasoning is creating some issues and reaching out to your feelings. Recognize and notice your concerns. Try not to attempt to overlook, battle, or control them like you normally would. All things being equal, just notice them as though according to an untouchable's point of view, without responding or judging. Let your concerns go. Notice that when you don't attempt to control the genuine fears that spring up, they before long pass, similar to mists getting across the sky. It's just when you connect with your concerns that you stall out. Remain fixed on the present. Focus on the manner in which your body feels, the beat of your breathing, your always evolving feelings, and the contemplations that float across your brain. In the event that you end up stalling out on a specific idea, take your consideration back to the current second. Rehash day to day. Utilizing care to keep fixed on the present is a straightforward idea, yet it requires investment and ordinary practice to receive the rewards. From the beginning, you'll presumably find that your brain holds meandering back to your concerns. Make an effort not to get disappointed. Each time you move your concentration back to the present, you're supporting another psychological propensity that will assist you with breaking liberated from the negative concern cycle.

Chapter 5

Always use positive self talk

Positive self-talk it's normal for the greater part of us to keep a running exchange inside our heads.
This discourse can go from giving ourselves directions while we complete an errand, to irregular perceptions about our current circumstance or a circumstance, or it very well may be what is frequently alluded to as self-talk. Self-talk is the inside story you hold about yourself. It's your inward voice and you might possibly have invested a lot of energy mulling over everything or really focusing on it. Truly, our self-talk can impact the manner in which we see ourselves, and our general surroundings than we understand. Before you read on, we figured you could get a kick out of the chance to download our 3 Self-Compassion Exercises for nothing. These definite, science-based activities

won't just assist you with expanding the empathy and generosity you show yourself however will likewise give you the devices to assist your clients, understudies or workers with showing more sympathy for themselves.

A Look at the Psychology Self-talk is for the most part remembered to be a blend of cognizant and oblivious convictions and inclinations that we hold about ourselves and the world by and large. It was Sigmund Freud who previously made the possibility that we have both cognizant and oblivious degrees of thought, with oblivious mental cycles affecting our conduct in manners we don't understand Self-talk can be positive or negative - and focusing on which you most frequently influence towards, can assist you with beginning rolling out proactive improvements about how you take on life's difficulties.

Negative Self-Talk Our examples of self-talk are time after time negative - we center around assumptions that we're 'not sufficient or 'consistently a disappointment' or 'can do nothing right. Our cerebrums are designed to recollect negative encounters over certain ones, so we review the times we didn't exactly hit the nail on the head more than the times we do. We then replay these messages to us, fuelling gloomy sentiments

Positive Self-Talk Positive self-talk, as you might have speculated, is the flip of negative self-talk. There's no need to focus on self-absorption, or misleading ourselves into thinking wrong things. It's more about showing yourself some self-empathy and understanding for what your identity and you've had to deal with Positive self-talk sees our inward story changing to thoughts like 'I can improve sometime later or 'I decide to gain from my slip-ups, not be kept down by them. What Does the Research Say? As far as how effective positive self-talk can be, the examination collectively concurs it's a considerable amount. From sports experts to getting thinner, to combatting melancholy: impacting the manner in which you converse with yourself can significantly affect conduct changes.) led a review where they asked patients with anorexia nervosa to stroll through an entryway that turned out to be progressively smaller. Members with the problem started to turn their bodies when the entryway was 40% more extensive than their shoulders, contrasted with members who had no conclusion, who possibly started to turn when the entryway was 25% more extensive than their shoulders. The scientists gathered that the negative self-talk the anorexic members partook in emphatically affected the manner they saw their bodies - causing them to accept they were bigger than they were. Conroy and Metzler (2004) investigated the manners in which self-talk influences mental uneasiness in sports execution. They took a gander at state-explicit self-talk, so the manner in which competitors addressed themselves while falling flat, while prevailing while at the same time wanting for progress, and keeping in mind that dreading disappointment. They estimated these close by articulations of circumstance explicit quality execution nervousness: apprehension about disappointment, feeling of dread toward progress, and game tension. They found the most grounded results for self-talk related with dread of disappointment and sports uneasiness, basically the competitors experienced higher tension while utilizing negative self-talk. Additionally, Kendall and Treadwell (2007) likewise investigated the manners in which self-talk influences nervousness. They examined self-talk as an indicator of tension in youngsters with and without a finding of an uneasiness issue. They found that decreasing negative self-talk intervened significant treatment acquires in youngsters with a finding.

Wrisberg (1993) found that self-talk can assist with further developing learning execution, by helping with the idea of 'piecing' complex data, which has been demonstrated in supporting review and doing complex assignments precisely. Chopra (2012) tracked down that giving understudies powerful techniques to transform negative self-talk into positive self-talk empowered them to effectively change their negative manners of thinking and the benefit of doing as such in their lives. Todd, Oliver, and Harvey (2011) evaluated the writing and exploration encompassing self-talk and consistently observed that positive self-talk intercessions are successful in intervening mental and conduct change.

The Importance and Benefits of Positive Self-Talk: Boost confidence As the exploration recommends, positive self-talk is significant in light of multiple factors. From assisting with defeating body dysmorphia to sports execution, intervening nervousness and discouragement, to more powerful learning: positive self-talk can improve things significantly.

Three extra advantages include:

1. Assists with diminishing Stress: Research has shown that individuals who are more disposed towards thinking hopefully, are likewise more leaned toward positive self-talk and use more dynamic survival techniques when confronted with upsetting circumstances and difficulties (Iwanaga, Yokoyama, and Seiwa, 2004). Positive self-talk helps you rethink the manner in which you take a gander at upsetting circumstances, understanding that you will move toward difficulties overall quite well and that whatever the result - you did all that could be expected. Handling these circumstances with an 'I can do this' outlook as opposed to a negative 'This is an excessively hard one, opens up better approaches for thinking and critical thinking.

2. Assists with supporting Confidence and Resilience: Approaching existence with a positive self-talk approach can assist with helping your fearlessness. People who score profoundly for hopefulness and positive confidence are bound to accomplish their objectives, score passing marks, and recuperate rapidly from a medical procedure (Lyubormisky, 2008). Standard good self-talk can assist you with feeling more positive about the essence of accomplishing your objectives, as you impart yourself with the conviction that the things you need are feasible, and when issues do emerge, you find workarounds.

3. Assists Build With bettering Relationships You're presumably mindful of what it seems like to associate with somebody positive, confident, and content in their identity personally. They radiate certainty, and it thinks about decidedly everyone around them. Assad, Donnellan, and Conger

(2012) observed that couples who were more hopeful refered to more elevated levels of collaboration and positive results. Individuals who use positive self-talk are additionally incredibly equipped for getting on the positive qualities of everyone around them. Is There any Evidence that Suggests it can Help with Anxiety and Depression? The exploration appears to help the possibility that positive self-talk can to be sure assist with messes like uneasiness and sorrow. This is principally on the grounds that negative self-talk has been broadly connected with problems like wretchedness, nervousness, low confidence, animosity, and post-horrible pressure problem (Leung and Poon, 2001, Owens and Chard, 2001).

Flipping self-converse with positive has likewise been displayed to intercede a few incredible outcomes with youngsters determined to have a nervousness problem (Kendall and Treadwell, 2007).

Everything this says to us is that positive self-talk can assist with beating these problems, by amending the predisposition towards negative contemplations and convictions we could hold about ourselves. Might it at any point Help Combat Stress? Basically, yes. As addressed momentarily, one of the advantages of positive self-talk is that it can assist you approach difficulties and distressing circumstances with a more open and hopeful mentality (Iwanaga, Yokoyama, and Seiwa, 2004). Positive self-talk isn't tied in with knowing every one of the responses or believing you're astounding, it's essentially about rethinking how you view things, eliminating negative predisposition, and moving toward existence with the possibility that you can handle things - and regardless of whether it go impeccably - you'll gain from it for sometime later.

www.ingramcontent.com/pod-product-compliance
Lightning Source LLC
LaVergne TN
LVHW052058160826
845678LV00015B/3281